The Nature and Science of
BUBBLES

Jane Burton and Kim Taylor

Gareth Stevens Publishing
MILWAUKEE

For a free color catalog describing Gareth Stevens Publishing's list of high-quality books and multimedia programs, call 1-800-542-2595 (USA) or 1-800-461-9120 (Canada). Gareth Stevens Publishing's Fax: (414) 225-0377.
See our catalog, too, on the World Wide Web: http://gsinc.com

Library of Congress Cataloging-in-Publication Data

Burton, Jane.
The nature and science of bubbles / by Jane Burton and Kim Taylor.
p. cm. -- (Exploring the science of nature)
Includes index.
Summary: Explains how, why, and where bubbles are formed and describes their different uses and various appearances.
ISBN 0-8368-1939-X (lib. bdg.)
1. Bubbles--Juvenile literature. [1. Bubbles.] I. Taylor, Kim. II. Title.
III. Series: Burton, Jane. Exploring the science of nature.
QC183.B935   1998
530.4'275--dc21   97-30214

First published in North America in 1998 by
Gareth Stevens Publishing
1555 North RiverCenter Drive, Suite 201
Milwaukee, Wisconsin 53212 USA

This U.S. edition © 1998 by Gareth Stevens, Inc. Created with original © 1997 by White Cottage Children's Books. Text and photographs © 1997 by Jane Burton and Kim Taylor. The photographs on page 8 (right), 9, 16, and 27 are by Mark Taylor. The photograph on page 17 is by Robert Burton. Conceived, designed, and produced by White Cottage Children's Books, 29 Lancaster Park, Richmond, Surrey TW10 6AB, England. Additional end matter © 1998 by Gareth Stevens, Inc.

The rights of Jane Burton and Kim Taylor to be identified as the authors of this work have been asserted by them in accordance with the Copyright, Design and Patents Act 1988. Educational consultant, Jane Weaver; scientific adviser, Dr. Jan Taylor.

Printed in the United States of America

1 2 3 4 5 6 7 8 9 02 01 00 99 98

Contents

Words that appear in the glossary are printed in **boldface**
type the first time they occur in the text.

Why Are Bubbles Round?

Bubbles form when a gas is released into a liquid. Usually, the gas is air and the liquid is water. But gas bubbles also form in other materials, such as red-hot **molten** metal or molten glass.

When an underwater bubble floats to the surface, it does one of two things — it either bursts and disappears or it floats. A floating bubble is quite different from a bubble under the water. It not only has gas inside it, but also outside it.

Bubbles tend to be round except when they are in contact with each other or with a solid object. Then they can have flat surfaces.

Bubbles are round because they are pulled into shape by a force called **surface tension**. Surface tension acts like an invisible piece of elastic on the surface of all liquids. A bubble floating in the air has both an inside and an outside surface, so there are two surface tension forces pulling it into a round shape.

Opposite: The larger of these oxygen bubbles are pushed toward the surface by the **pressure** of the water. But they are also held back by the green weed that produced them. So instead of being round, they are pear-shaped.

Below: Floating bubbles are attracted to solid objects and to each other. When they touch an object, bubbles can have flat sides, like these bubbles resting against the glass of an aquarium.

Bubbles in Water

Green plants in sunlight release oxygen, which is a gas. When plants in the water release oxygen, the gas forms bubbles. Strings of little oxygen bubbles can be seen slowly rising from the stems or leaves of water weed in ponds and aquariums. Bigger bubbles rise more quickly. Large bubbles of **methane** sometimes even come rushing to the surface. Methane, or marsh gas, forms under water when dead plant material rots.

Small bubbles are held in a round shape by surface tension. But surface tension is not strong enough to hold bigger bubbles in shape. Big bubbles flatten or turn into mushroom shapes and may even break up into smaller bubbles as they wobble up to the surface.

Right: Underwater bubbles trapped beneath ice press against the underside of the ice. These methane bubbles rose to the surface at intervals as the lake was freezing. During the time between one bubble rising and the next, the ice thickened, causing columns of bubbles to form inside the ice.

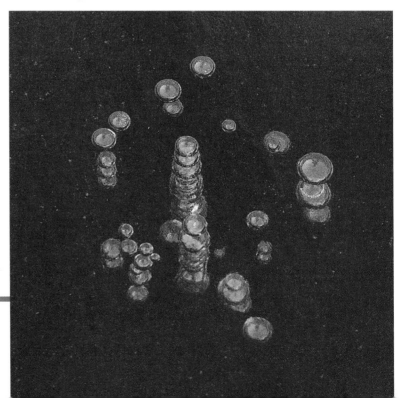

Left: Mud at the bottom of a lake often contains trapped methane gas. The slightest disturbance will cause the gas to bubble up to the surface. As this avocet walks delicately through the shallow water, a trail of methane bubbles forms behind.

The size of a bubble in water depends on pressure. The deeper the water, the greater the pressure. The greater the pressure, the smaller the bubble. A huge, crushing pressure exists at the bottom of the ocean because of the enormous weight of the water. In this area, a lot of gas is squeezed into a very little space. A bubble the size of a pea in the ocean depths would swell to the size of a football by the time it reached the surface — if it did not break up into thousands of smaller bubbles along the way.

Above: The small bubbles on this water lily have not come from the plant but from the water itself. They are bubbles of air that dissolved in the water overnight and then reappeared as the water warmed in the morning.

Opposite: Old Faithful, the famous geyser in Yellowstone National Park in the Rocky Mountains, takes about an hour to build enough pressure to erupt.

Right: In some parts of the world, water near the surface of Earth heats to a boil due to the hot rocks underneath. The pool of boiling water pictured has steam bubbles rising from it.

Bubbles sometimes appear in water as if from nowhere. Clear water left standing in a glass may contain several little bubbles on the sides of the glass after a few minutes. These are made of air that was dissolved in the water. The bubbles form when the water warms because warm water can hold less dissolved air than cold water. Bubbles also form when pressure is reduced. For instance, when you turn on a faucet, the water that comes out is under less pressure than it was in the pipe — so bubbles often form in fresh tap water.

The bubbles in boiling water are not air but steam. In some parts of the world, hot rocks deep underground heat water to the boiling point. The water comes bursting to the surface in the form of a geyser. Bubbles of steam in the underground water expand because the pressure falls as the water comes rushing upward. This causes the geyser to squirt high into the air.

Bubbles Out of Water

Bubbles that rise in a pond or river usually burst when they reach the surface. But sometimes a bubble will float, and you can see that it is formed from a thin layer of water. A large floating bubble is almost a **hemisphere**. Where its edge sits on the water, surface tension pulling inward is balanced by gas pressure pushing outward, keeping the bubble in its shape.

Detergent in the water makes floating bubbles last longer. Some **polluted** rivers contain detergents, and that is why there are often masses of bubbles floating on the surface.

Below: A large raindrop rushes down toward the surface of a pond.

The raindrop smacks into the surface, sending up a circular sheet of water shaped like a crown.

The force of the raindrop causes a round pit to form in the surface, while the crown-shaped sheet rises still higher.

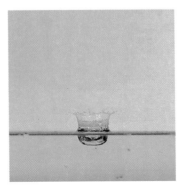

Left: Worms and shrimp live in burrows on muddy seashores. The burrows become filled with air at low tide. When the tide comes in, this air is forced out, forming large, floating bubbles.

Detergents reduce surface tension. This means that the pulling force on the surface of bubbles is reduced, so the bubbles do not burst as easily. That is why it is possible for people to blow round bubbles that float through the air out of water that contains a little detergent.

Surface tension acts like a drawstring and begins to pull the top of the crown-shaped sheet inward.

The top of the crown is pulled together by the surface tension, forming a bubble. Part of the bubble is the pit in the water's surface.

As the effect of the drop's force wears off, water at the bottom of the pit rushes upward, forming a column that shoots up through the top of the bubble.

Breathing Bubbles

Opposite: A water spider keeps a silvery-looking supply of air trapped among the hairs of its body so it can breathe under water. It also spins an underwater bell of silk. The spider brings air down to the bell and fills it with a large bubble. This makes a safe place for the air-breathing spider to rest while it looks for prey.

Animals that live in water but breathe air have to keep returning to the surface for air. But many of these smaller creatures carry a bubble of air with them so they don't have to come to the surface as often. Some water beetles keep air under their **elytra**, or wing cases. Other beetles have hairs on their undersides that hold a bubble of air. These beetles can stay under water for several minutes, or even hours, using their breathing bubbles. Newts and frogs come to the surface to gulp air into their lungs. While under water, they hold their breath.

Some animals that breathe in water come onto land occasionally. They have to bring enough water with them to keep their **gills** wet. Crabs that come onto land take in some air to supply the water around their gills with oxygen. When they blow this air out, bubbles often form.

Top and right: The great diving beetle is an air-breather. When it dives, this beetle takes a supply of air with it, stored under its elytra cases.

Whales and dolphins come to the surface regularly to take deep breaths so they can store large amounts of oxygen in their blood and muscles. They breathe out again before they dive but still take some air with them.

Under the water, dolphins communicate with each other in the form of squeaks. With each squeak, a thin stream of bubbles comes out of a dolphin's **blowhole**.

Whales also produce bubbles. A group of whales will swim in a circle below a school of fish. Each whale then lets out a stream of bubbles. As the bubbles rise, they form a circular curtain through which the fish do not like to swim. Then the whales can easily eat the fish.

Above: Dolphins are air-breathing mammals. This one has just come to the surface of the sea to breathe. Its blowhole, or nostril, takes in air.

Right: Just before a dolphin surfaces, it empties its lungs of old air. The air bursts out of its blowhole as a mass of bubbles.

Humans cannot hold their breath for more than two or three minutes at a time. This means divers must take an air supply with them when they go under water. A diver working in deep water breathes air that is under great pressure. This pressure causes nitrogen gas to dissolve in the diver's blood. When the diver comes to the surface and the pressure is released, little bubbles of nitrogen may form in the blood. This causes a painful — and sometimes fatal —condition called **diver's bends**. A whale does not suffer from the bends because it does not breathe under water. It holds its breath.

Below: Whales take several deep breaths before each dive. This makes sure that their blood is well supplied with oxygen while they are feeding under water. With each breath, a cloud of spray and **condensation** rises in the air. Here, two whales spout close to each other.

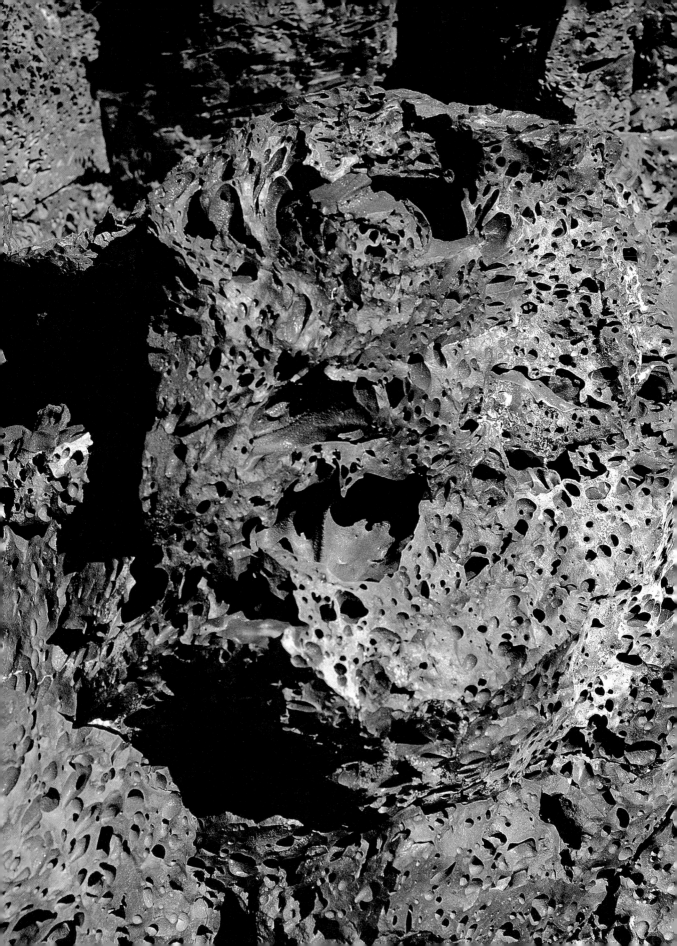

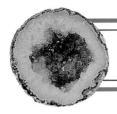

Frozen Bubbles

Bubbles form in liquids only. But liquids can harden, which traps the bubbles. When molten lava, or liquid rock, erupts high into the air out of volcanoes, the pressure inside the lava is released very suddenly. The lava becomes frothy and cools quickly. This frothy rock is called pumice. It is so light that chunks of it can float on water.

Bubbles that rise to the surface of a body of water as it freezes are trapped beneath the ice. The ice sheets in Greenland and Antarctica are hundreds of feet (meters) thick and contain air bubbles that were trapped many thousands of years ago. By drilling deep holes in the ice and collecting air from these bubbles, scientists can tell what Earth's **atmosphere** was like long ago.

Top: A **geode** is a hollow ball of rock, like a big bubble of gas set in rock. Inside, beautiful crystals of purple amethyst grow.

Opposite: Red-hot molten lava is very thick and sticky, and gas bubbles often become trapped in it. The lava cools and transforms into rock that is full of holes.

Left: Water is a clear liquid. It freezes into ice, which is a clear solid. Yet **icebergs** look bluish white, not clear. This is because most ice is filled with many little bubbles. The bubbles scatter light that passes through the ice, making the ice appear to be bluish white.

17

Bubble Wrap

Top: This male Siamese fighting fish takes in a bubble of air at the water's surface. Siamese fighting fish make nests for their eggs by spitting out a mass of mucus-coated bubbles.

For some creatures, such as spittlebugs (frog-hoppers), a mass of bubbles makes a good hiding place and provides protection from enemies. Spittlebugs are small hopping insects that live on plants. Their **nymphs** are soft and delicate and cannot yet hop around. If left unprotected, the nymphs would make tasty morsels for other animals. The spittlebug nymphs blow blobs of small bubbles made from plant juice, in which they hide. Hundreds of these bubble blobs can be seen on grasses and flowering plants in spring.

Some animals wrap their eggs or young in bubbles to protect them. Tree frogs lay their eggs on twigs that hang over ponds. The frogs produce slime when they are laying the eggs. They kick their hind legs in the slime, which forms bubbles. The eggs then hang in this mass of sticky white froth that protects them. The **tadpoles** hatch into the froth and swim around in it for a while before dropping into the pond below.

Left: The praying mantis lays its eggs in a mass of froth that dries into a tough material. The hardened froth protects the eggs over winter. The young hatch in spring.

Left and **above:**
A spittlebug nymph feeds on plant **sap**. It uses its **proboscis** to pierce the stem of the plant. Spittlebug nymphs draw more sap than they need for food. They use the extra to form a mass of bubbles in which to hide from enemies.

Bubbles Make Floats

Top: Egg or knotted wrack has large **bladders** to buoy up its thick, rubbery **fronds**.

Many water animals use bubbles as floats to keep themselves on the surface or to hang midway in the water. Phantom midge **larvae** have a pair of bubbles at each end so that their bodies hang in the water. Violet sea snails use slime to blow a small collection of tough bubbles that keeps the snails floating on the surface of the sea. Another sea creature called Portuguese man-of-war is able to float on the water because of its clear, bubble-like body. In the wind, Portuguese men-of-war blow around on top of the water with their **tentacles** trailing in the water.

Right: Portuguese men-of-war are related to jellyfish. They have transparent bladders that float on the surface of the water. The Portuguese men-of-war pictured have washed ashore among some seaweed.

Left: The fronds of bladder wrack contain many oxygen-filled bladders. These support the plant in the water so that, when the tide comes in, the fronds float upright.

Strictly speaking, the Portuguese man-of-war's body is not a bubble because it is not made from a liquid. It is a bladder formed of a thin layer of elastic substance that is blue in color. A balloon is a good example of a bladder. Some seaweeds, such as bladder wrack, collect oxygen in bladders. Their fronds float up over the rocky seabed when the tide comes in.

Below: Phantom midge larvae have nearly transparent bodies. They hang motionless in freshwater pools, waiting for prey. Their bodies are supported by two pairs of air bubbles, one near the head and one near the tail.

Being able to hang in mid-water is useful for fish. They can rest without fear of sinking to the bottom. Most fish can adjust their **density** so that it is the same as that of water. Their bodies hold a bubble of oxygen inside what is known as a **swim bladder**. Fish use the oxygen dissolved in their blood to control the size of this bubble. The bubble's size determines whether the fish will sink or rise in the water.

Gases can be **compressed**, so when a fish dives into deeper water, its swim bladder is squeezed smaller. The fish then has to pump more oxygen into the swim bladder in order to stay the same density as the water. The floating power of a bubble is related to its size, not the amount of gas in it. Squeeze a big bubble (or bladder) into a smaller space, and it will not float as well.

Opposite: These African lake fish rise, sink, or remain motionless in the water simply by adjusting the amount of oxygen in their swim bladders.

Below: These common frogs float at the surface of a pond, breathing air.

When the frogs dive, they expel some air bubbles so that it is easier for them to swim to the bottom of the pond.

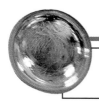

Looking into Bubbles

Top: A floating bubble formed by a raindrop acts as a mirror.

Opposite: The bubbles in this stream are lenses through which reduced images of the plants and gravel below can be seen. If you look very carefully, you may see images of little yellow fish in some of the bubbles.

A bubble under the water is a kind of **lens**. If you look through a bubble that has formed on the side of a glass of water, you can see in it a greatly reduced, somewhat **distorted**, image of the objects beyond and the sky above.

Bubbles in water often look silvery in color. The image of the sky makes the tops of the bubbles look that way.

Floating bubbles and soap bubbles in the air are not lenses. They simply act as curved mirrors, reflecting a distorted image of the objects that are around them.

Fascinating colors can be seen in soap bubbles, depending on the thickness of the film of water that forms the bubble. A freshly formed bubble is thick and has no colors. As the bubble grows, its wall stretches and becomes thinner. Then green and red colors appear. The bubble will continue to get thinner because water **evaporates** from it. It will become yellow, blue, and purple before it bursts.

Left: This floating bubble reflects a distorted image of its surroundings and has rainbow colors.

Bubble Baths

Top: A fiddler crab takes in air to supply the water around its gills with oxygen. When the crab blows the air out, some of the water comes out as well, forming bubbles.

Wherever there is water, there are almost always bubbles. Even in a still pool, strings of tiny bubbles often rise from the bottom. A rushing river with waterfalls is full of bubbles. In certain areas of a rushing river, bubbles make the water look white. Waves in a rough sea also make masses of bubbles. Sometimes these form froth on the surface that the wind then picks up and carries inland.

Bubbles are the result of liquid and gas coming together, and surface tension is the vital force that allows them to form. Surface tension tries to make all bubbles round. But other forces pull or push bubbles out of the round shape or break them into smaller bubbles.

Right: Breaking waves cause pure white foam to form in clean seawater. The bubbles making up the foam may last only a few seconds before they burst. This is because the surface tension of seawater is fairly high. Gray seals can be seen coming ashore through the breakers.

Some water animals carry with them their own bubble of air for breathing, while some land animals hide in frothy balls of bubbles. Fish use gas bubbles in their swim bladders to regulate their depth in the water. But people use bubbles mostly just for baths and fun!

Above: A huge waterfall, like Niagara Falls in New York and Ontario, makes plenty of foam. But the foam does not last long. The bubbles burst as they travel downstream.

Activities:

Playing with Bubbles

Bubble Colors

Water has no color. The soap or detergent added to water to do dishes or laundry may simply give the water a faint green or yellow tinge. Yet, whenever a bubble forms in the mixture, beautiful rainbow colors appear. Where do these colors come from? The answer lies in the nature of light.

To study the colors in bubbles, you need a short plastic drinking glass, a small disposable plastic container (such as a film canister without the lid), liquid soap, and water. *Ask an adult to help you carefully punch several holes in the bottom of the*

Below: The wall of this bubble is thin at the top, but gets thicker toward the bottom, causing bands of color.

canister. Half fill the plastic drinking glass with water, and add a tiny bit of liquid soap to it. Mix well, and get ready to blow bubbles.

Briefly dip the open end of the canister in the mixture and then blow through the bottom where you made the holes to make a bubble. Note that when the bubble starts to form, there is no color. As you continue blowing, reds and greens appear. At this stage, free the bubble by moving the canister quickly sideways. The longer the bubble lasts, the more colorful it becomes.

A cold day is better than a warm day for blowing bubbles because your warm breath inside the bubbles causes them to rise in the cold air. They may even go sailing over the rooftops!

A red and green bubble hanging in the air on a bright, cold morning is a wonderful sight. Gradually, its color changes to yellow, then blue, and purple. Finally, it may be completely colorless again, or holes may seem to appear in it shortly before it bursts. The reason for these color changes is that water is constantly evaporating from the bubble, causing its wall to get thinner. The thickness of a bubble's wall determines its color.

Light from the Sun is made up of all the colors of the rainbow mixed together. Each color has a slightly different **wavelength**. When the thickness of the bubble's wall matches the wavelength of a particular color, that color is reflected by the bubble instead of passing through it, and so that color is visible. The waves of light are no farther apart than the thickness of a

bubble's wall — a tiny distance. So, as water evaporates and the bubble's wall thins, the longest wavelength of light (red) is reflected first and the shortest wavelength (purple) last. When holes seem to appear in the bubble or it stops reflecting altogether, the wall has become so thin that visible light passes straight through. Only ultraviolet light is reflected. Humans cannot see ultraviolet light, but some insects and birds can.

Above: A negative bubble is made of a thin film of air in water. It is not filled with air but contains a blob of water.

Negative bubbles

A soap bubble is a thin film of water floating in the air. Would it be possible to have the opposite — a thin film of air floating in water? This does not seem possible, but it is. **Negative bubbles**, as they are called, do exist, although they are never very big.

To make a negative bubble, you need a large, clear glass or plastic container in which to form the negative bubbles; a spoon; a small pitcher; liquid soap; and water. Fill the container with water, and add a little soap. Dip the pitcher into the container, and fill it with soapy water. Hold the spoon the right way up just above the surface of the water in the container and gently pour water into it from the pitcher (*above, right*). Vary the height of the spoon above the water and the flow from the pitcher until silvery beads of water start to skate over the surface. Eventually, some of these beads will get pushed beneath the surface of the water, taking a film of air with them and forming the mysterious and elusive negative bubbles.

The bubbles drift only slowly toward the surface and look different from normal underwater bubbles. Like soap bubbles in air, they do not form lenses.

When a negative bubble bursts, a few small air bubbles race upward toward the surface. This is just the opposite of what happens when a soap bubble bursts in the air. Then, a few small drops of water race downward toward the ground.

Below: An air bubble, trapped in the clear jelly of frog spawn, works as a lens, producing small images of the growing tadpoles.

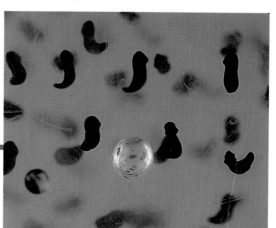

Glossary

atmosphere: the layer of air and clouds that surrounds Earth.

bladder: a bag that can be filled with gas or liquid.

blowhole: a hole on the top of the head of whales, dolphins, and porpoises through which these animals breathe.

compress: to squeeze into a smaller space.

condensation: a condition in which water comes out of the air in the form of droplets.

density: the amount of matter in an object. (A stone is much denser than a cork, for example.)

distorted: twisted out of normal shape or condition.

diver's bends: a dangerous and painful condition experienced by divers who come to the surface of the water too quickly.

elytra: the hardened forewings under which beetles keep their folded hind wings. (Singular: elytrum)

evaporate: to change from liquid to vapor.

frond: a long leaf or leaf-like structure.

geode: a hollow ball of rock that often contains crystals on its inner surface.

gills: organs used by water animals for breathing.

hemisphere: half of a round, ball-shaped object or sphere.

iceberg: a huge block of ice, once part of a glacier or ice shelf, that floats in the sea.

larvae: the early stages in the growth of some animals. (Singular: larva)

lens: a piece of clear material with curved sides that focuses light.

methane: a gas made from carbon and hydrogen.

molten: liquefied by heat.

negative bubble: a bubble formed of a thin film of air in water.

nymph: the young and normally wingless stage of many kinds of insects.

polluted: a condition when water, air, soil, or some other substance is filled with toxins and rubbish.

pressure: the application of force to an object.

proboscis: the tube-like mouthpart of some insects.

sap: the liquid found inside plants that contains nourishing food for the plants.

surface tension: the layer at the surface of a liquid that acts like stretched, elastic material.

swim bladder: a gas-filled bag inside a fish that controls its depth in water.

tadpole: the larva of frogs, toads, newts, and salamanders.

tentacles: thin, wavy arms on the bodies of some animals. The tentacles are used for grasping or gathering food.

wavelength: the distance between similar points on waves.

Plants and Animals

The common names of plants and animals vary from language to language. But plants and animals also have scientific names, based on Greek or Latin words, that are the same the world over. Each plant and animal has two scientific names. The first name is called the genus. It starts with a capital letter. The second name is the species name. It starts with a small letter.

Adélie penguin (*Pygoscelis adeliae*) — Antarctica *17*

Amazon sword plant (*Echinodorus paniculatus*) — South America *25*

avocet (*Recurvirostra avosetta*) — Europe, Africa *7*

bladder wrack (*Fucus vesiculosus*) — North Atlantic shores *21*

blue whale (*Balaenoptera musculus*) — Atlantic and Pacific oceans *14-15*

butterfly fish (*Pantodon bulchholzi*) — West Africa *8*

common dolphin (*Delphinus delphis*) — seas worldwide *14*

common frog (*Rana temporaria*) — Europe *23*

egg or knotted wrack (*Aescophyllum nodosum*) — North Atlantic shores *20*

fanwort (*Cabomba aquatica*) — South America *25*

goldfish (*Carassius auratus*) —domesticated, kept worldwide *Cover*

gray seal (*Halochoerus grypus*) — North Atlantic coasts *26*

great diving beetle (*Dytiscus marginalis*) — Europe *12, 31*

lemon tetra (*Hyphessobrycon pulchripinnis*) — South America *25*

nasturtium (*Tropaeolum majus*) — South America, cultivated worldwide *10*

phantom midge (*Chaoborus crystallinus*) — Europe *20-21*

praying mantis (large) (*Paratenodera ardifolia*) — Japan *18*

rock crab (*Leptograpsus variegatus*) — Australia *1*

Siamese fighting fish (*Betta splendens*) — Malay Peninsula and Thailand *18*

spittlebug (*Philaenus spumarius*) — Europe *18-19*

water spider (*Argyroneta aquatica*) — Europe *12-13*

yellow cichlid (*Neolamprologus leleupi*) — East Africa *22*

Books to Read

Bubblemania. Penny R. Durant (Avon)
Bubbles. Bernie Zubrowski (Little, Brown)
Experiments With Bubbles. Robert Gardner (Enslow Publications)
The Science of Soap Films and Soap Bubbles. Cyril Isenberg (Dover)

Soap Bubble Magic. Seymour Simon (Lothrop, Lee & Shepard)
Soap Science: A Science Book Bubbling with 36 Experiments. J. L. Bell (Addison-Wesley)
Tom Noddy's Bubble Magic. Tom Noddy (Running Press)

Videos and Web Sites

Videos

Floating and Sinking. (Journal Films)
Learning About Water. (AIMS Media)
Water. (Barr Films)
Water and What It Does. (Encyclopædia
 Britannica Educational Corporation)
Water You Up To? (Media, Inc.)

Web Sites

www.rescol.ca/collections/science_world/
 english/projects/activities/bubbles.html
www~ocean.tamu.edu//Quarterdeck/
 QD3.3/Lyons/lyons.html
bubbles.org/
www.sln.org

Index